little hands
SEEDS

Rachel Matthews

All kinds of plants grow from seeds.

Seeds grow into trees, flowers, fruit, and vegetables.

3

Seeds vary in size, shape, weight, and color.

radish

orange

apple

cherry

cress

grape

Collect some different seeds.
What do they look and feel like?

marigold

plum

oak (acorn)

sycamore

horse chestnut (buckeye)

5

Pour small seeds into a pot with a lid.

Put large seeds in another pot.

What color and shape are the seeds?

Shake each pot.

What different sounds do
the seeds inside make?

The outside of this seed is smooth and firm.

Inside this seed is a tiny plant waiting to grow.

What happens when you plant a seed?

Put a seed in a
pot of damp soil.
Gently cover
the seed
with soil.

Put the pot in a light place.
Make sure the soil stays damp.

A plant is beginning to grow from the seed!
Can you see the green shoot?

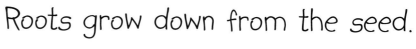

Roots grow down from the seed.

A growing plant sucks up water through its roots.

When a plant has flowered, it leaves seeds behind.

Often the seeds are protected inside a fruit or pod.

This pole bean holds the seeds inside.

Collect some fruits and vegetables. Look inside them.

cucumber

kiwi fruit

pear

tomato

pomegranate

Some have many tiny seeds. Others have just one big seed.

avocado

cherry

papaya

pepper

squash

17

Plants scatter their seeds in different ways.

Light seeds are blown by the wind.

Seeds are food for many animals.
They spread seeds by storing and eating them.

People eat seeds, too.

We cook with them and eat them raw.

Which of these seeds have you tasted?

coffee

sunflower

poppy

orchid (vanilla)

rice

pumpkin

sesame

Make a seedcake for birds to eat.

Stir some seeds
into melted
vegetable fat.
Ask an adult
to help you.

Notes for teachers and parents

Pages 2-3

Discussion: Encourage the children to discuss their experience of seeds. They may have noticed sesame seeds on top of hamburger buns or have a pet hamster that eats seeds. They may prefer seedless grapes to grapes with pips inside.

Activity: To introduce the connection between seeds and the germination and growth of flowering plants, you could invite a gardener to talk to the children about growing plants from seed. You could plant some seeds in the classroom. The children could make and illustrate their own seed packets.

Pages 4-5

Seeds can vary greatly in size, shape, and appearance, e.g. a chestnut in its spiky case is a seed, as is a pea in a pod, an avocado stone, and an orange pip.

Activity: Collect examples of seeds and ask the children to describe each one and explain how it differs from another, e.g. "This seed is round, smooth, shiny, and brown while that seed is smaller and flatter, and it's green."

Pages 6-7

Activity: If available, let the children experiment with musical instruments that use seeds to make sounds, e.g. coconut shells, shakers, and rainmakers (seed-filled tubes which replicate the sound of falling rain).

Pages 8-9

Explain that a seed's hard outer layer protects the plant inside which will begin to grow when the conditions are right.

Experiment: Soak a bean seed overnight, remove its outer coating, and cut it open to show children the embryonic plant inside.

Pages 10-13

Planting seeds allows children to explore the conditions necessary for germination.

Activity: Cress seeds germinate reliably and can be grown on damp blotting paper so the children can see what is happening. Each child could try planting some seeds in the shape of his or her name or initials.

Experiment: Investigate what happens when seeds are left unwatered. Encourage the children to deduce that water is needed for seeds to germinate. Put one set of germinated seeds on a window sill and another in a dark cupboard. Comparing the progress of the two sets, the children should notice that plants need light as well as water to grow and flourish.

Pages 14-17

Introduce the idea of a life cycle of a flowering plant, from seed to flower to seed-filled "fruit."

Activity: Show the children a flowering plant (removed from its pot), and point out the different parts: roots, stem, leaves, and the flowers with their petals.

Activity: Show the children the "ripe" seed pod (the fruit) of a plant such as a petunia. The children could try shaking the pod over a paper bag to collect the seeds.

Pages 18-19

Link the need for a plant to spread its seeds to its life cycle.

Discussion: Study a range of seeds, e.g. on a dandelion head, in a poppy seed-head, inside a melon, or on the surface of a strawberry. Can the children suggest some ways in which the seeds might be dispersed?

Pages 20-22

Many seeds are good for us as they contain healthy food for a growing plant.

Activity: Make a list of seeds the children have come across at home and at school. Point out ones that the children may not have thought of as seeds, such as coffee and rice.

Discussion: Remind the children that not all seeds are safe to eat. Tell them to check with an adult before touching or tasting any seeds that are new to them.

Index

animals	19, 22	planting	10–11
color	4–6	root	13
comparing	4–5, 16–17	scattering seeds	18–19
describing	4-5, 7	shape	4–6
eating	19–21	shoot	12
flowers	3, 5, 14	size	4–6, 16–17
fruit	3–5, 15–17	sounds	6–7
grow	2–3, 9, 12–13	trees	3, 5
inside (seeds)	9	vegetables	3–4, 15–17
pod	15		

This U.S. edition copyright © 2006 Chrysalis Education
Published in conjunction with Chrysalis Books Group Plc.

International copyright reserved in all countries.
No part of this book may be reproduced in any form
without written permission from the publisher.

Distributed in the United States by
Smart Apple Media
2140 Howard Drive West
North Mankato, Minnesota 56003

Library of Congress Control Number: 2004108788

ISBN 1-59389-212-8

Associate publisher: Joyce Bentley
Project manager and editor: Penny Worms

Art director: Sarah Goodwin
Designer: Patricia Hopkins
Picture researchers: Veneta Bullen, Miguel Lamas
Photographer: Ray Moller

The author and publishers would like to thank the following people for their
contributions to this book: Ruth Thomson, Jack Bell, Mollie Worms and
Mollie Parker.

Printed in China

10 9 8 7 6 5 4 3 2 1

Picture acknowledgements
All reasonable efforts have been made to ensure the reproduction of content
has been done with the consent of copyright owner. If you are aware of any
unintentional omissions please contact the publishers directly so that any
necessary corrections may be made for future editions.

Getty Images: Markus Essler 19.